Making a Difference

HARCOURT BRACE SOCIAL STUDIES

READING SUPPORT
AND TEST PREPARATION

HARCOURT BRACE & COMPANY

Orlando Atlanta Austin Boston San Francisco Chicago Dallas

New York Toronto London

Visit The Learning Site at http://www.hbschool.com

Printed in the United States of America

ISBN 0-15-312376-1

6 7 8 9 10 073 01 00

Contents

Introduction

The articles in *Reading Support and Test Preparation* relate to the units in Harcourt Brace's *Making a Difference*. There are two articles for each unit. The articles have been designed to provide high-interest, motivating reading experiences that expand on or spring from a person's life, an event, or a topic that is presented in the unit. In most instances, the articles contain some of the vocabulary words from the unit so that children have an opportunity to reinforce key vocabulary.

There are a number of ways that you can use the articles. You may wish to use the articles after you have completed the unit in *Making a Difference*, in which children are exposed to background information about the topic. You may also use the articles before children read the unit, as a way to provide background. You may want to read aloud the articles to children, or you may wish to have children use the articles as a test simulation experience.

Each article is preceded by a three-part, A-B-C Lesson Plan (Access, Build, and Close), which provides a simple procedure for using the article. A Word Splash or an Anticipation Guide blackline master is included with the plan for children to use before reading the article. These copying masters can be used to help build interest, activate prior knowledge, and set purposes for reading. The lesson plan also includes a related cross-curricula activity in language arts, mathematics, science, or art.

For Units 1, 2, and 4, there is an Activity Master at the end of each article. This Activity Master gives children an opportunity to respond to the article and sum up the main idea of it. For Units 3, 5, and 6, there are six comprehension questions at the end of each article. The questions assess reading skills and strategies, such as identify the best summary, identify the main idea, and draw conclusions.

Item analyses and answer keys are provided at the back of the book to assist you with evaluation. Also at the back of this book are descriptions of several useful reading comprehension strategies that you can use with the articles. Several blackline masters of word webs and charts suitable for duplication are also included.

Harcourt Brace School Publishers

Reading Support and Test Preparation has been designed to provide

- additional motivating reading experiences for your children.
- content related to units in *Making a Difference.*
- opportunities to build background and reinforce reading skills.
- practice opportunities for standardized tests.
- reading strategy activities to help children organize information.

CONVERSION CHART FOR SCORING

After children have read the article and answered the questions,
you can use the following chart to determine a grade.

Correct Number of Responses	Percentage Score
6	100%
5	83%
4	67%
3	50%
2	33%
1	17%

Davy Crockett

A·B·C LESSON PLANNER

1. Access

- **READING STRATEGY:** Use the Word Splash on page 2 to help children make predictions about the article. Write the words on the board, or use the sheet as a copying master. Invite children to predict how each word or phrase relates to Davy Crockett. Children can write or draw their predictions in their journals or learning logs. Do not expect children to know the answers. This activity is designed to help build interest, activate prior knowledge, and set purposes for reading.

2. Build

- Have children read the article, or read it aloud to them.

- As children read or after they finish reading the article, they may change their Word Splash predictions. Have them identify the predictions that were correct, and have them state what they have learned from reading the article.

3. Close

- Have children complete the copying master *Remember Davy Crockett.* Invite children to list in the outline some of the things Crockett did.

- **SCIENCE ACTIVITY:** Have children research the kinds of animals Davy Crockett might have hunted in Tennessee. Invite children to list the animals.

Harcourt Brace School Publishers

Name_____

Davy Crockett

Word Splash

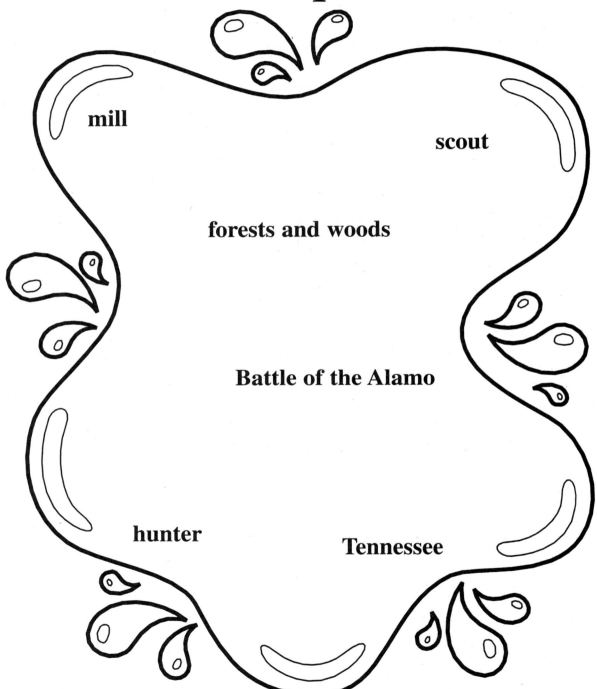

mill

scout

forests and woods

Battle of the Alamo

hunter

Tennessee

Harcourt Brace School Publishers

Name _____

Davy Crockett

Davy Crockett grew up in a family that loved the outdoors. When Davy was eight years old, his family moved to Cove Creek, Tennessee. There, his father built a mill. Davy was too young to work in the mill. He spent his time in the woods. As he grew older, he learned to hunt. His father gave him one bullet a day. He told Davy to hunt only for food or for skins and not to waste his shots. Later, Davy said that he became a good hunter because he learned to shoot with only one bullet a day.

Davy Crockett was an **explorer,** or a person who searches for new places to learn about. He had an exciting life as an explorer, a hunter, and a woodsman. He was a scout in the Creek Indian Wars. He was also a member of Congress.

Davy Crockett died in Texas at the Battle of the Alamo, bravely fighting to protect the fort against the Mexican Army. Today, Davy Crockett has a place in history and in the many tall tales that are told about him.

Name_____

Remember Davy Crockett

What to do: Write or draw some of the things Davy Crockett did.

Scouting Experiences

A·B·C LESSON PLANNER

1. Access

• **READING STRATEGY:** Use the Word Splash on page 6 to help children make predictions about the article. Write the words on the board, or use the sheet as a copying master. Invite children to predict how each word or phrase relates to scouting activities. Children can write or draw their predictions in their journals or learning logs. Do not expect children to know the answers. This activity is designed to help build interest, activate prior knowledge, and set purposes for reading.

2. Build

• Have children read the article, or read it aloud to them.

• As children read or after they finish reading the article, they may change their Word Splash predictions. Have them identify the predictions that were correct, and have them state what they have learned from reading the article.

3. Close

• Have children complete the copying master *A Special Badge.* Invite children to design a badge for something they would like to learn to do.

• **LANGUAGE ARTS ACTIVITY:** Have children write a letter to a local Scouting organization to invite a leader or spokesperson to come talk to the class.

Scouting Experiences

Word Splash

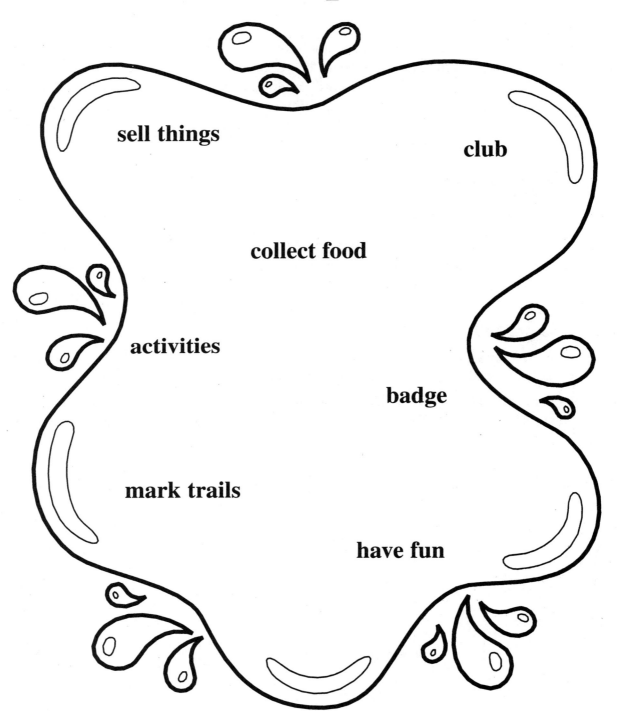

sell things

club

collect food

activities

badge

mark trails

have fun

Name _____

Scouting Experiences

Many boys and girls enjoy Scouting. The Scouts are clubs for boys and girls. Girls from six to eight years old can join Brownies. Boys from six to ten years old can join Cub Scouts.

In Brownies and Cub Scouts, boys and girls learn to do many things. Some Scouting activities are outdoors, such as learning to mark a trail. Other activities include sewing and cooking. For each activity that a Scout completes, he or she gets a badge. The badge shows that the Scout knows how to do something special. Scouts wear uniforms and attend regular meetings.

Some Scouts sell things to earn money for their clubs. They may sell cookies or candy. With the money they collect, they support their clubs. Scouts also collect food for people who live in shelters.

There are Scouting clubs for older boys and girls, too. Older boys join the Boy Scouts. Older girls join the Girl Scouts. These clubs teach boys and girls how to do many things and give them a chance to have fun together.

Name_____

A Special Badge

What to do: Draw a design for a badge for something you want to learn to do.

Harcourt Brace School Publishers

Native American Homes

A·B·C *L*ESSON *P*LANNER

1. *A*ccess

- **READING STRATEGY:** Use the Word Splash on page 10 to help children make predictions about the article. Write the words on the board, or use the sheet as a copying master. Invite children to predict how each word or phrase relates to Native American homes. Children can write or draw their predictions in their journals or learning logs. Do not expect children to know the answers. This activity is designed to help build interest, activate prior knowledge, and set purposes for reading.

2. *B*uild

- Have children read the article, or read it aloud to them.

- As children read or after they finish reading the article, they may change their Word Splash predictions. Have them identify the predictions that were correct, and have them state what they have learned from reading the article.

3. *C*lose

- Have children complete the copying master *A Native American Home.* Invite children to draw a kiva with wall paintings.

- **SCIENCE ACTIVITY:** Have children research the mesas of the Southwest. Invite children to write three facts that they find.

Name_____

Native American Homes
Word Splash

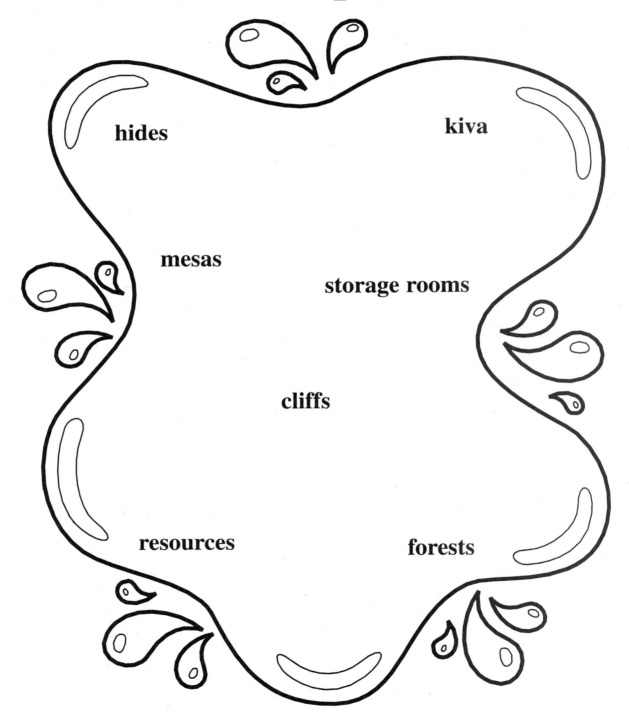

hides

kiva

mesas

storage rooms

cliffs

resources

forests

Name_____

Native American Homes

Native Americans used resources from the land around them to make their homes. The Cheyenne lived in an area where there were many buffalo. They used buffalo hides to make their houses. The Iroquois lived near forests. They used wood to make their homes.

Some Native Americans living in what is now Arizona used the cliffs and mesas of their area for their homes. They built houses with many rooms in the sides of cliffs. These houses had storage rooms for grain. They also had rooms for eating and sleeping.

A special room was called a kiva. Some Native Americans used this room for religious ceremonies. This room was mainly underground. It was entered through a hole dug in the ground. The men of the village climbed down a ladder to enter the kiva. The walls of the kiva had many paintings on them. There might be a fire in the middle of the kiva for warmth.

Where Native Americans lived was important to them. They depended on the land for many things. They used what they found on the land to build the kinds of homes they needed.

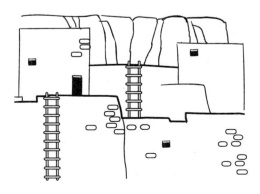

Name_____

A Native American Home

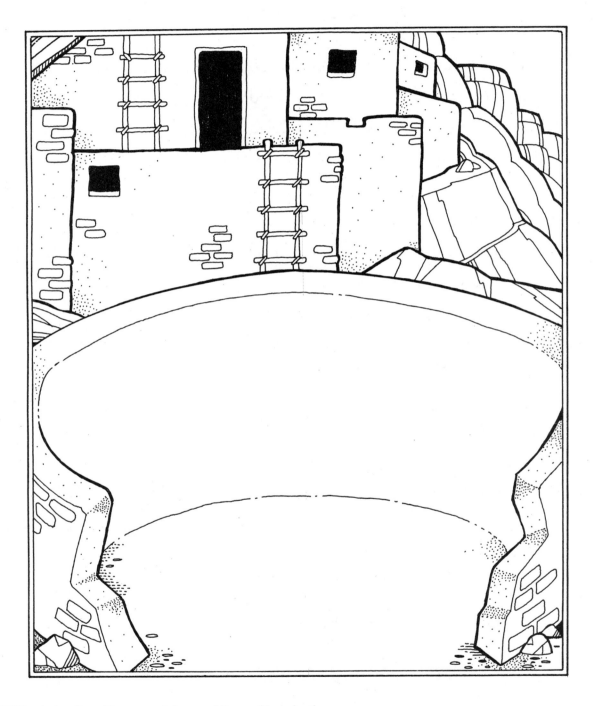

What to do: Draw a kiva with wall paintings.

Storyteller Dolls

A·B·C LESSON PLANNER

1. Access

- **READING STRATEGY:** Use the Word Splash on page 14 to help children make predictions about the article. Write the words on the board, or use the sheet as a copying master. Invite children to predict how each word or phrase relates to storyteller dolls. Children can write or draw their predictions in their journals or learning logs. Do not expect children to know the answers. This activity is designed to help build interest, activate prior knowledge, and set purposes for reading.

2. Build

- Have children read the article, or read it aloud to them.
- As children read or after they finish reading the article, they may change their Word Splash predictions. Have them identify the predictions that were correct, and have them state what they have learned from reading the article.

3. Close

- Have children complete the copying master *My Storyteller*. Invite children to draw the children who are listening.
- **LANGUAGE ARTS ACTIVITY:** Have children work in small groups to plan a story to tell to the class. Invite children to select one member of each group to tell the story. The others can play the parts of the listeners.

Name_____

Storyteller Dolls

Word Splash

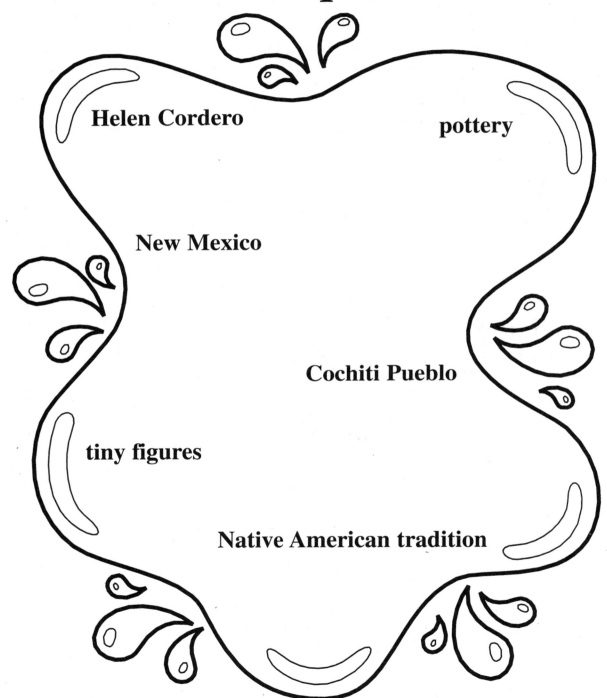

Helen Cordero

pottery

New Mexico

Cochiti Pueblo

tiny figures

Native American tradition

Harcourt Brace School Publishers

Name _____

Storyteller Dolls

Certain groups of Native Americans have made storyteller dolls since the late 1800s. These dolls are made out of **pottery,** or baked clay. The storyteller is usually seated with his or her legs outstretched. The storyteller's head is thrown back, and his or her mouth is wide open. The storyteller is telling a story.

Tiny figures are climbing all over the storyteller. These are the children who are listening to the story. Some are in the storyteller's lap. Some are even climbing up the storyteller's back. The faces of the children show happiness or alarm, depending on the story.

In the late 1950s, Helen Cordero began to make storyteller dolls. Helen Cordero was from the Cochiti Pueblo, or group of Native Americans, in New Mexico. Her storyteller dolls were based on her grandfather.

Today, many artists from the Pueblos of New Mexico make storyteller dolls. Each artist has his or her own style of doll. The dolls all celebrate storytelling, an important Native American tradition.

Name_____

My Storyteller

What to do: Here is the storyteller. Think about what kind of story he or she is telling. Draw the children who are listening.

Let's Trade

A·B·C *LESSON PLANNER*

1. *Access*

- **READING STRATEGY:** Use the Anticipation Guide on page 18 before having small groups of children read the article. Write the statements on the board, or use the sheet as a copying master. Invite children to tell whether they agree or disagree with each statement. They can write or draw their responses in their journals or learning logs. Do not expect children to know the answers. This activity is designed to help build interest, activate prior knowledge, and set purposes for reading.

2. *Build*

- Have children read the article, or read it aloud to them.
- As children read or after they finish reading the article, they may change their opinions about the statements. If they do, have them discuss why they revised their opinions and have them state what they learned from their reading that allowed them to confirm or revise their opinions.

3. *Close*

- Have children complete the standardized-test-format questions after they read the article. (An item analysis that identifies the test objectives covered by each question, as well as an answer key, can be found on page 49.)
- **MATHEMATICS ACTIVITY:** Have groups of children discuss some of the trade items in the article. Invite children to assign prices to the items. Then encourage children to use the prices to write number problems for members of the group to solve.

Name_____

Let's Trade

Anticipation Guide

	Agree	Disagree
1. People used to trade things they had for things they needed.		
2. Some people thought feathers were worth a lot.		
3. People who had nothing to trade went hungry.		
4. People still trade today.		
5. Things that are traded for each other are usually worth different amounts.		

Harcourt Brace School Publishers

Name _____

Let's Trade

Step back in time and picture a world without money. There are no dollar bills. There are no coins. How can a person get food or clothing?

In the past, people traded things they had for things they needed or wanted. Items that were traded were thought to be worth about the same amount. People might trade ten chickens for a pig. They might trade some sugar for a bowl or a cup.

Some groups of people thought certain items were **valuable,** or worth a lot. In the Santa Cruz Islands, people thought that feathers were valuable. They glued together tiny red feathers and traded with them. Some North American Indians made belts out of beads. They called the belts wampum. They traded them for things they wanted. In Ethiopia people traded rock salt for the things they wanted.

How did people who did not have much to trade get the things they wanted? Sometimes people would trade their skill. They might fix someone's roof to get a place to sleep. They might help care for someone's animals to get food for their families.

Today, people still trade for things other than money. A sister might help her younger brother with his homework if he agrees to make her bed. There is no limit to what can be traded.

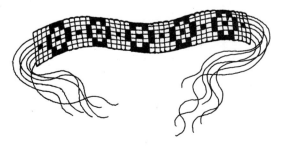

Name_____

Let's Trade

Choose the best answer and mark the oval of your choice.

1. Which of these is the best summary for this article?
   - ⬭ People today use money.
   - ⬭ People trade things to get what they want or need.
   - ⬭ Ten chickens are worth one pig.
   - ⬭ Beads and feathers can be worth a lot.

2. Why do people trade things?
   - ⬭ They have a lot of one thing.
   - ⬭ They want to be friendly.
   - ⬭ It is the law.
   - ⬭ They want to get the things they need.

3. In this article, the word **valuable** means
   - ⬭ worth a lot.
   - ⬭ having a lot.
   - ⬭ given to someone else.
   - ⬭ making yourself.

4. What did the people in Ethiopia trade?
   - ⬭ They traded rock salt.
   - ⬭ They traded beads.
   - ⬭ They traded feathers.
   - ⬭ They traded shells.

5. What is the main idea of the fourth paragraph?
   - ⬭ People have many skills.
   - ⬭ People can trade their skills for what they need.
   - ⬭ People who can fix a roof can become rich.
   - ⬭ Trading is hard work.

6. Which of these is a fact presented in the article?
   - ⬭ Everyone trades every day.
   - ⬭ People who have a lot of money never trade.
   - ⬭ People still trade goods or skills for things they want.
   - ⬭ Friends always trade with each other.

Harcourt Brace School Publishers

Lick and Stick

A·B·C *L*ESSON *P*LANNER

1. *Access*

- **READING STRATEGY:** Use the Word Splash on page 22 to help children make predictions about the article. Write the words on the board, or use the sheet as a copying master. Invite children to predict how each word or phrase relates to postage stamps. Children can write or draw their predictions in their journals or learning logs. Do not expect children to know the answers. This activity is designed to help build interest, activate prior knowledge, and set purposes for reading.

2. *Build*

- Have children read the article, or read it aloud to them.

- As children read or after they finish reading the article, they may change their Word Splash predictions. Have them identify the predictions that were correct, and have them state what they have learned from reading the article.

3. *Close*

- Have children complete the standardized-test-format questions after they read the article. (An item analysis that identifies the test objectives covered by each question, as well as an answer key, can be found on page 49.)

- **ART ACTIVITY:** Have children work with a partner to design a new stamp. Children may wish to choose an animal, flower, or person from their state for the stamp. Invite children to present their stamps to the class and to explain why they chose the image they did.

Name_____

Lick and Stick

Word Splash

adhesive

collection

Benjamin Franklin

England

George Washington

Harcourt Brace School Publishers

Lick and Stick

Think about this riddle: **I can be a rectangle or a square. You find me on envelopes in your mailbox. What am I?** I am a postage stamp!

Postage stamps let the mail carrier know that someone has paid to send a piece of mail from one place to another. The kinds of stamps people use today have been around for over 100 years.

The first **adhesive** stamps were sold in May 1840, in England. These stamps were stuck onto the envelope. There were two stamps— a one-cent stamp and a two-cent stamp.

Stick-on stamps were very popular. People used them for mail, and they saved them in collections.

The United States made its first stick-on stamps in 1847. The five-cent stamp had a picture of Benjamin Franklin on it. The ten-cent stamp had a picture of George Washington.

Now there are many kinds of stamps in the United States. Some stamps cost one cent, and others cost one dollar or even more. Many stamps have pictures of famous people who have died on them. There are also stamps with pictures of flowers and special places.

Some stamps are pretty and colorful. That is why lots of people like to collect stamps. There is even a national stamp collection. It is in the Smithsonian Institution, in our nation's capital.

Name_____

Lick and Stick

Choose the best answer and mark the oval of your choice.

1. Which of these is the best summary for this article?
   - ⬭ Stamps did not cost very much in the past, and they do not cost much today.
   - ⬭ People use stamps for their mail, and many people like to collect them.
   - ⬭ All of the old stamps were worth one cent or two cents.
   - ⬭ Stamps have always had pretty pictures on them.

2. In this article, the word **adhesive** means
   - ⬭ stick-on.
   - ⬭ postage.
   - ⬭ envelopes.
   - ⬭ stamps.

3. The first stick-on stamps were sold in
   - ⬭ May 1804.
   - ⬭ July 1776.
   - ⬭ May 1997.
   - ⬭ May 1840.

4. Benjamin Franklin was on the
   - ⬭ one-cent U.S. stamp.
   - ⬭ five-cent U.S. stamp.
   - ⬭ one-cent English stamp.
   - ⬭ two-cent English stamp.

5. What is the main idea of the sixth paragraph?
   - ⬭ Some stamps have pictures of flowers.
   - ⬭ Stamps can cost one cent.
   - ⬭ There are many kinds of stamps.
   - ⬭ Pictures of famous buildings are often found on stamps.

6. How do you know the Smithsonian Institution is in Washington, D.C.?
   - ⬭ It has a national stamp collection.
   - ⬭ It is a big museum.
   - ⬭ It is far from where you live.
   - ⬭ It is in our nation's capital.

Sacagawea

A·B·C *L*ESSON *P*LANNER

1. *A*ccess

- **READING STRATEGY:** Use the Word Splash on page 26 to help children make predictions about the article. Write the words on the board, or use the sheet as a copying master. Invite children to predict how each word or phrase relates to Sacagawea. Children can write or draw their predictions in their journals or learning logs. Do not expect children to know the answers. This activity is designed to help build interest, activate prior knowledge, and set purposes for reading.

2. *B*uild

- Have children read the article, or read it aloud to them.

- As children read or after they finish reading the article, they may change their Word Splash predictions. Have them identify the predictions that were correct, and have them state what they have learned from reading the article.

3. *C*lose

- Have children complete the copying master *Follow the Route*. Invite children to color the route taken by Lewis and Clark.

- **ART ACTIVITY:** Show children pictures of the kinds of canoes that Sacagawea and Lewis and Clark might have used on their journey. Invite children to draw the canoes.

Name_____

Sacagawea
Word Splash

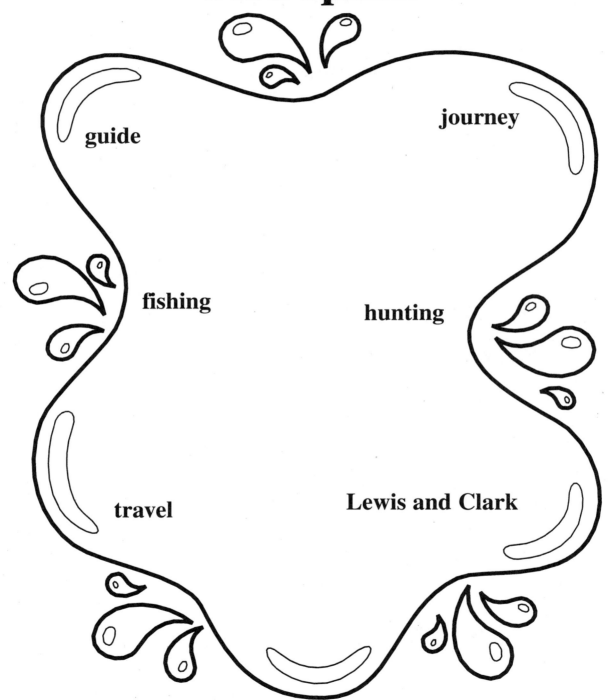

guide

journey

fishing

hunting

travel

Lewis and Clark

Harcourt Brace School Publishers

Sacagawea

Sacagawea is remembered in history because she was part of a great adventure. She was the guide who led two explorers across the mountains to the Oregon coast. The two explorers were Meriwether Lewis and William Clark. White men had not explored much of this land before Lewis and Clark set out.

Before Sacagawea began her journey with Lewis and Clark, she had many adventures. As a child she liked hunting and fishing. She wanted to ride horses as her brother did. She learned to swim and did many other things. She was always exploring.

Sacagawea was ready to help Lewis and Clark when they asked her. She wanted to see parts of the country that her people had not seen before. She was ready for the trip.

Today, in North Dakota, there is a statue of Sacagawea and her baby. There is also a statue of her in Portland, Oregon. These statues honor Sacagawea for her role in the journey with Lewis and Clark.

Harcourt Brace School Publishers

Name_____

Follow the Route

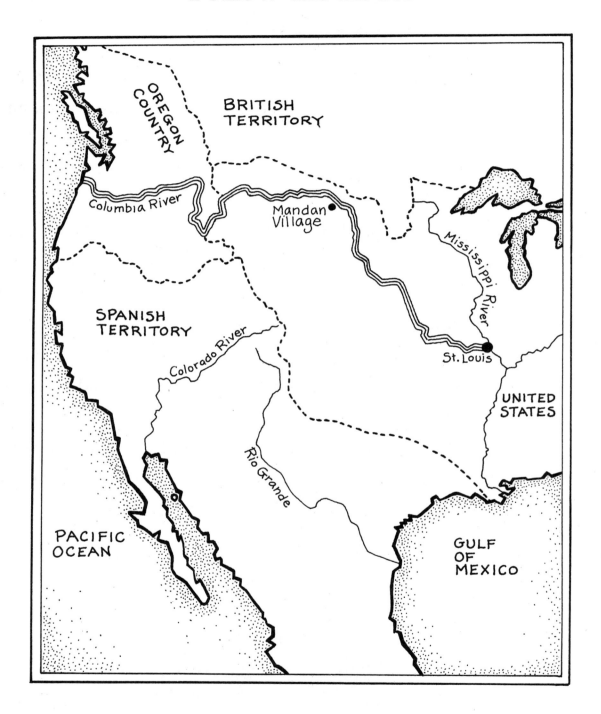

What to do: Color the route taken by Lewis and Clark.

The *Mayflower*

A·B·C *L*ESSON *P*LANNER

1. *Access*

- **READING STRATEGY:** Use the Word Splash on page 30 to help children make predictions about the article. Write the words on the board, or use the sheet as a copying master. Invite children to predict how each word or phrase relates to the *Mayflower*. Children can write or draw their predictions in their journals or learning logs. Do not expect children to know the answers. This activity is designed to help build interest, activate prior knowledge, and set purposes for reading.

2. *Build*

- Have children read the article, or read it aloud to them.

- As children read or after they finish reading the article, they may change their Word Splash predictions. Have them identify the predictions that were correct, and have them state what they have learned from reading the article.

3. *Close*

- Have children complete the copying master *The Mayflower Log.* Invite children to draw or write what the voyage might have been like.

- **LANGUAGE ARTS ACTIVITY:** Have children imagine that they are passengers on the *Mayflower.* Have each child write or draw a journal entry for the day that they first see land. Children can share their entries.

Harcourt Brace School Publishers

Name_____

The <u>Mayflower</u>
Word Splash

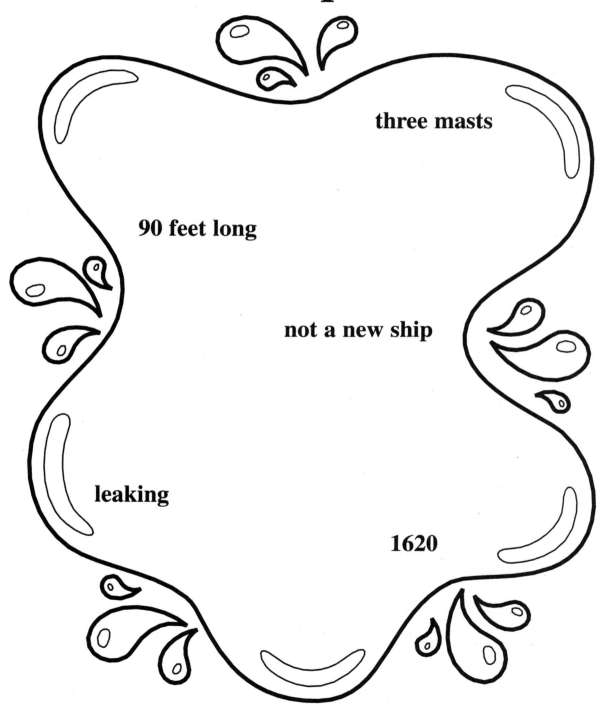

three masts

90 feet long

not a new ship

leaking

1620

Harcourt Brace School Publishers

The Mayflower

In 1620, about 100 passengers sailed to America to find a new life. They sailed on a ship called the <u>Mayflower</u>. The <u>Mayflower</u> was not a new ship. It had been used by the English in many trading voyages before it set sail for America. Some historians think that the <u>Mayflower</u> had been used to fight sea battles with Spain.

The <u>Mayflower</u> was 90 feet long from stem to sternpost. It had three masts for sails. It was armed with several cannons. On each side of the ship were openings for the cannons to shoot from.

One of the sailors on the <u>Mayflower</u> called the ship a "leaking, unwholesome ship." The voyage on the <u>Mayflower</u> was not an easy one. The people who made the voyage wanted a new life badly. That was why the long voyage was worth it to them. Today, we know how brave the Pilgrims were to make the trip.

Name_____

The <u>Mayflower</u> Log

What to do: Draw or write what the voyage on the <u>Mayflower</u> might have been like.

State Nicknames

A·B·C *L*ESSON *P*LANNER

1. *A*ccess

- **READING STRATEGY:** Use the Word Splash on page 34 to help children make predictions about the article. Write the words on the board, or use the sheet as a copying master. Invite children to predict how each word or phrase relates to states and their nicknames. Children can write or draw their predictions in their journals or learning logs. Do not expect children to know the answers. This activity is designed to help build interest, activate prior knowledge, and set purposes for reading.

2. *B*uild

- Have children read the article, or read it aloud to them.

- As children read or after they finish reading the article, they may change their Word Splash predictions. Have them identify the predictions that were correct, and have them state what they have learned from reading the article.

3. *C*lose

- Have children complete the standardized-test-format questions after they read the article. (An item analysis that identifies the test objectives covered by each question, as well as an answer key, can be found on page 49.)

- **LANGUAGE ARTS ACTIVITY:** Have children work with a partner to come up with some other nicknames for their state. Invite children to think of qualities, resources, or geographical features of the state that could be used in the nicknames.

Name_____

State Nicknames

Word Splash

Rhode Island

Grand Canyon State

California

Sunshine State

Lone Star State

official name

Name _____

State Nicknames

Many people are given one name when they are born but are also called by another, shorter name. This other name is a **nickname.**

In the United States, states have official names and nicknames. For example, Texas is the official name given to the Lone Star State, which is its nickname.

Many of our states' official names come from Native American languages. Alabama's name comes from the Choctaw. Alaska's name comes from the Aleuts. Some other states honor important people in the history of our country. The state of Washington is named for the country's first president.

Some states choose nicknames to show off a natural feature or resource. Arizona is called the Grand Canyon State. New Hampshire is called the Granite State. California is called the Golden State. Other states choose nicknames to make tourists want to visit the state. Florida is called the Sunshine State. Rhode Island is called the Ocean State.

Most states answer to more than one nickname. Michigan is known as the Wolverine State and the Great Lakes State. Minnesota is called the North Star State, the Gopher State, and the Land of 10,000 Lakes.

Whatever their official name, states are proud of their nicknames, too.

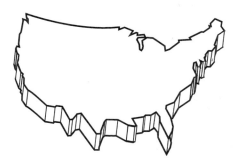

Name_____

State Nicknames

Choose the best answer and mark the oval of your choice.

1. Which of these is the best summary for this article?
   - ⬭ People have interesting nicknames.
   - ⬭ States' nicknames tell something about the state.
   - ⬭ Many states have more than one nickname.
   - ⬭ Nicknames are often funny.

2. In this article, the word **nickname** means
   - ⬭ a name different from an official or birth name.
   - ⬭ an exciting name.
   - ⬭ a name that tells about the United States.
   - ⬭ a name that all people like.

3. What is the nickname for California?
   - ⬭ the Lone Star State
   - ⬭ the Sunshine State
   - ⬭ the Granite State
   - ⬭ the Golden State

4. What is the main idea of the fourth paragraph?
   - ⬭ Everyone must like a state's nickname.

   - ⬭ Some states choose nicknames based on features or resources in their state.
   - ⬭ All states have resources.
   - ⬭ States choose nicknames based on the size of their state.

5. Which of these is a fact presented in the article?
   - ⬭ Texas has the best nickname in the country.
   - ⬭ People love nicknames that make them laugh.
   - ⬭ Florida is called the Sunshine State.
   - ⬭ It is better to have more than one nickname for a state.

6. Why do states have more than one nickname?
   - ⬭ Other states already have their nickname.
   - ⬭ People can't make up their minds.
   - ⬭ People keep forgetting the nickname.
   - ⬭ More than one nickname fits the state.

Harcourt Brace School Publishers

It's a Secret

A·B·C *L*ESSON *P*LANNER

1. *Access*

- **READING STRATEGY:** Use the Anticipation Guide on page 38 before having small groups of children read the article. Write the statements on the board, or use the sheet as a copying master. Invite children to tell whether they agree or disagree with each statement. They can write or draw their responses in their journals or learning logs. Do not expect children to know the answers. This activity is designed to help build interest, activate prior knowledge, and set purposes for reading.

2. *Build*

- Have children read the article, or read it aloud to them.

- As children read or after they finish reading the article, they may change their opinions about the statements. If they do, have them discuss why they revised their opinions and have them state what they learned from their reading that allowed them to confirm or revise their opinions.

3. *Close*

- Have children complete the standardized-test-format questions after they read the article. (An item analysis that identifies the test objectives covered by each question, as well as an answer key, can be found on page 50.)

- **MATHEMATICS ACTIVITY:** Have children count the number of students in the class. Then invite children to have an election of class officers. Encourage children to count the ballots for each candidate and tally the results.

Name_____

It's a Secret

Anticipation Guide

	Agree	Disagree
1. Every citizen has the right to vote in secret.		
2. Most adults vote by raising their hands.		
3. Everyone votes in a voting booth.		
4. When people fill out ballots, no one else can see what they are doing.		
5. Even the ancient Greeks voted in secret.		

It's a Secret

It's time to pick a class president. Will you cast your vote by raising your hand? Or will you write your choice on paper?

When adults in the United States cast their votes in an election, they do it in secret. This is so no one will know who another person votes for. It is a way of protecting people.

Some people vote in a voting booth. The voter closes a curtain so that he or she can vote in secret. On the back wall of the booth is a list of all the people the voter can vote for. The voter picks the candidate. When the voter is finished voting, he or she pulls a handle and moves it to one side. This tells the machine to count the vote. The first voting machines were used in 1892 in New York State.

Some people fill out a **ballot,** or sheet of paper. The voter stands in a small desk-like space that has a border on each side. No one can see how the voter is filling in his or her ballot. When the voter is finished voting, he or she puts the ballot through a machine and the vote is counted in secret. Paper ballots have been used in the United States since the late 1700s.

No matter how or where people vote in the United States, their votes are secret. That is an important right for every citizen of the United States.

VOTING BALLOT

Harcourt Brace School Publishers

Name_____

It's a Secret

Choose the best answer and mark the oval of your choice.

1. Which of these is the best summary for this article?
   - ⬭ Voting in secret is a right of every citizen of the United States.
   - ⬭ Some people vote in a voting booth.
   - ⬭ Some people vote by filling in a secret paper ballot.
   - ⬭ Colored balls were used for voting.

2. The first voting machines were used in
   - ⬭ New York City.
   - ⬭ Austin, Texas.
   - ⬭ the Republic of Texas.
   - ⬭ New York State.

3. In this article, the word **ballot** means
   - ⬭ a sheet of paper.
   - ⬭ a machine.
   - ⬭ a voting booth.
   - ⬭ a vote.

4. What is the main idea of the third paragraph?
   - ⬭ Some voters vote in a voting booth.
   - ⬭ Ballots are put through a machine.
   - ⬭ No one can see how a voter fills out a ballot.
   - ⬭ Some voters use a ballot to cast their votes.

5. Which of these is a fact presented in the article?
   - ⬭ People would rather vote in a voting booth.
   - ⬭ Black and white balls make good ballots.
   - ⬭ Paper ballots have been used in the United States since the late 1700s.
   - ⬭ Children vote by raising their hands.

6. How is voting in secret a way of protecting people?
   - ⬭ Voting booths make sure a person's vote is a secret.
   - ⬭ No one else can know how a person is voting.
   - ⬭ No one wants to know how another person votes.
   - ⬭ Secret ballot is the best way to vote.

Greetings!

A·B·C *L*ESSON *P*LANNER

1. *A*ccess

- **READING STRATEGY:** Use the Word Splash on page 42 to help children make predictions about the article. Write the words on the board, or use the sheet as a copying master. Invite children to predict how each word or phrase relates to greeting cards. Children can write or draw their predictions in their journals or learning logs. Do not expect children to know the answers. This activity is designed to help build interest, activate prior knowledge, and set purposes for reading.

2. *B*uild

- Have children read the article, or read it aloud to them.

- As children read or after they finish reading the article, they may change their Word Splash predictions. Have them identify the predictions that were correct, and have them state what they have learned from reading the article.

3. *C*lose

- Have children complete the standardized-test-format questions after they read the article. (An item analysis that identifies the test objectives covered by each question, as well as an answer key, can be found on page 50.)

- **ART ACTIVITY:** Have children work with a partner to design a greeting card for someone they know. Children may wish to create a birthday card or a card for another special occasion.

Name_____

Greetings!

Word Splash

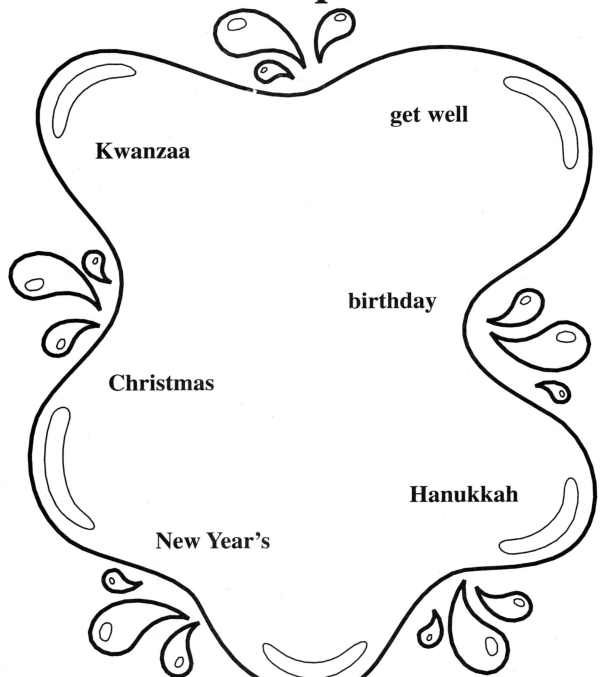

get well

Kwanzaa

birthday

Christmas

Hanukkah

New Year's

Greetings!

"Happy birthday!" "Get well soon!" People send greeting cards to one another each year for holidays and on other special days.

The people in Egypt over 4,000 years ago sent New Year's greetings and gifts to one another. The Romans would also send gifts.

Now, billions of cards are made and sold each year. More than half of them are Christmas cards. Many other holidays, such as Hanukkah and Kwanzaa, have special cards. Most of the other cards that are made are birthday cards. Other cards are made to help people say "Thank you," or "Feel better," or "Congratulations."

The first modern Christmas card was made in London, England. It was designed in 1843 by John C. Horsley, an artist. The card had three parts. In the center was a family having Christmas dinner. On one side the artist drew people feeding the hungry. On the other side was a picture of people giving clothes to poor families.

In the United States the first Christmas card was made in 1875. A printer named Louis Prang had a printing shop in Boston. He designed and sold the first color Christmas card in the country. Soon he was known as the father of the American greeting card.

There are many different kinds of cards today. Some play music. Others hold money or become games and puzzles. One thing hasn't changed, though—cards can still make people happy.

Greetings!

Choose the best answer and mark the oval of your choice.

1. Which of these is the best summary for this article?
   - ◯ Everyone enjoys receiving a birthday card.
   - ◯ There are many different greeting cards, and they can make people feel happy.
   - ◯ Many greeting cards are sold all over the United States.
   - ◯ Some greeting cards play music, hold money, and turn into games and puzzles.

2. Which of these is a fact presented in the article?
   - ◯ The Egyptians and the Romans were the first people to celebrate New Year's.
   - ◯ The Romans sent musical Christmas cards to friends.
   - ◯ The Egyptians sent New Year's gifts to one another.
   - ◯ All Egyptians received special New Year's gifts.

3. What is the main idea of the third paragraph?
   - ◯ There are special cards for Kwanzaa.
   - ◯ There are billions of cards for holidays and other special days.

   - ◯ Most people send birthday cards to each other every year.
   - ◯ There are only a few kinds of Christmas cards for people to send.

4. The first Christmas card was made in
   - ◯ London in 1843.
   - ◯ Boston in 1843.
   - ◯ Egypt, over 4,000 years ago.
   - ◯ the early Roman Empire.

5. Why was Louis Prang called the father of the American greeting card?
   - ◯ He was the father of many children.
   - ◯ His family had made greeting cards for many years.
   - ◯ The American Revolution started in Boston where Louis Prang lived.
   - ◯ He made the first Christmas card in the United States.

6. The most popular kind of greeting cards are for
   - ◯ Hanukkah.
   - ◯ Christmas.
   - ◯ birthdays.
   - ◯ Kwanzaa.

Stack 'em Up

A·B·C LESSON PLANNER

1. Access

- **READING STRATEGY:** Use the Anticipation Guide on page 46 before having small groups of children read the article. Write the statements on the board, or use the sheet as a copying master. Invite children to tell whether they agree or disagree with each statement. They can write or draw their responses in their journals or learning logs. Do not expect children to know the answers. This activity is designed to help build interest, activate prior knowledge, and set purposes for reading.

2. Build

- Have children read the article, or read it aloud to them.

- As children read or after they finish reading the article, they may change their opinions about the statements. If they do, have them discuss why they revised their opinions and have them state what they learned from their reading that allowed them to confirm or revise their opinions.

3. Close

- Have children complete the standardized-test-format questions after they read the article. (An item analysis that identifies the test objectives covered by each question, as well as an answer key, can be found on page 50.)

- **MATHEMATICS ACTIVITY:** Have children create recipe files for various pancake recipes. Invite children to record the precise measurements for all the ingredients.

Name_____

Stack 'em Up

Anticipation Guide

	Agree	Disagree
1. Pancakes are for breakfast only.		
2. People in many countries eat pancakes.		
3. Only butter and syrup can be put on pancakes.		
4. In some countries pancakes are filled with meat or vegetables.		
5. In China thin pancakes are made with just flour and water.		

Name _____

Stack 'em Up

What's for breakfast, or for lunch, or even for dinner? How about some yummy pancakes!

In the United States most people eat pancakes for breakfast. They are made from a mixture of flour, milk, eggs, and oil. Sometimes they also have sugar and baking powder in them. Then the thick **batter** is poured onto a hot griddle or pan. When little bubbles pop on the top of the pancakes, the cook flips them over for a minute or two. Then they are ready to eat with butter and syrup.

In France pancakes are called crepes (krayps). These pancakes are very thin. Crepes for lunch or dinner are usually filled with meat or vegetables. Other crepes filled with fruits or jams are used for dessert.

In China thin pancakes are made with just flour and water. The pancakes are cooked **quickly** in a pan, but only on one side. When they are done, the pancakes are filled with vegetables or meat.

In Mexico people eat tortillas (tor-TEE-yuz). These are made with wheat flour or with corn meal. They can be filled with meat, vegetables, or beans. Many people like cheese and spicy sauce with their tortillas, too.

There are special kinds of pancakes in other countries, too. Russia and India have their own special kinds. So no matter where you go, you can have delicious pancakes any time!

Stack 'em Up

Choose the best answer and mark the oval of your choice.

1. Which of these is the best summary for this article?
   - ⬭ People put all kinds of things on pancakes.
   - ⬭ Pancakes are a great break-fast food.
   - ⬭ People in Mexico eat tortillas.
   - ⬭ There are different kinds of pancakes all over the world.

2. In this article, the word **batter** means
   - ⬭ a mixture.
   - ⬭ a special type of pancake.
   - ⬭ a snack.
   - ⬭ a baseball player.

3. Which pancakes can be eaten for dessert?
   - ⬭ the French pancakes called crepes
   - ⬭ pancakes with honey
   - ⬭ cornmeal tortillas
   - ⬭ Chinese pancakes with a special sauce

4. In this article, the word **quickly** means
   - ⬭ in a warm way.
   - ⬭ in a fast way.
   - ⬭ in a slow way.
   - ⬭ in a cold way.

5. Which of these is a fact presented in the article?
   - ⬭ Tortillas are the pancakes that taste the best.
   - ⬭ Chinese pancakes are the easiest pancakes to make.
   - ⬭ Tortillas are made with wheat flour or with corn meal.
   - ⬭ Corn meal tortillas are better than flour tortillas.

6. Why might so many people in so many countries like to eat pancakes?
   - ⬭ They are easy to make.
   - ⬭ They taste good.
   - ⬭ They can be made in a pan or in the oven.
   - ⬭ They are cooked.

ITEM ANALYSES AND ANSWER KEYS

Unit 3

LET'S TRADE

Item Analysis: 1. Identify the best summary; 2. Identify cause and effect; 3. Identify specialized/technical terms; 4. Recall supporting facts and details; 5. Identify the main idea; 6. Distinguish between fact and nonfact.

Answers: 1. People trade things to get what they want or need. 2. They want to get the things they need. 3. worth a lot. 4. They traded rock salt. 5. People can trade their skills for what they need. 6. People still trade goods or skills for things they want.

LICK AND STICK

Item Analysis: 1. Identify the best summary; 2. Use context clues; 3. Recall supporting facts and details; 4. Recall supporting facts and details; 5. Identify the main idea; 6. Make inferences and generalizations.

Answers: 1. People use stamps for their mail, and many people like to collect them. 2. stick-on. 3. May 1840. 4. five-cent U.S. stamp. 5. There are many kinds of stamps. 6. It is in our nation's capital.

Unit 5

STATE NICKNAMES

Item Analysis: 1. Identify the best summary; 2. Identify specialized/technical terms; 3. Recall supporting facts and details; 4. Identify the main idea; 5. Distinguish between fact and nonfact; 6. Draw conclusions.

Answers: 1. States' nicknames tell something about the state. 2. a name different from an official or birth name. 3. the Golden State. 4. Some states choose nicknames based on features or resources in their state. 5. Florida is called the Sunshine State. 6. More than one nickname fits the state.

IT'S A SECRET

Item Analysis: 1. Identify the best summary; 2. Recall supporting facts and details; 3. Identify specialized/technical terms; 4. Identify the main idea; 5. Distinguish between fact and nonfact; 6. Draw conclusions.

Answers: 1. Voting in secret is a right of every citizen of the United States. 2. New York State. 3. a sheet of paper. 4. Some voters vote in a voting booth. 5. Paper ballots have been used in the United States since the late 1700s. 6. No one else can know how a person is voting.

Unit 6

GREETINGS!

Item Analysis: 1. Identify the best summary; 2. Distinguish between fact and nonfact; 3. Identify the main idea; 4. Recall supporting facts and details; 5. Make inferences and generalizations; 6. Recall supporting facts and details.

Answers: 1. There are many different greeting cards, and they can make people feel happy. 2. The Egyptians sent New Year's gifts to one another. 3. There are billions of cards for holidays and other special days. 4. London in 1843. 5. He made the first Christmas card in the United States. 6. Christmas.

STACK 'EM UP

Item Analysis: 1. Identify the best summary; 2. Identify specialized/technical terms; 3. Recall supporting facts and details; 4. Identify prefixes and suffixes; 5. Distinguish between fact and nonfact; 6. Make inferences and generalizations.

Answers: 1. There are different kinds of pancakes all over the world. 2. a mixture. 3. the French pancakes called crepes. 4. in a fast way. 5. Tortillas are made with wheat flour or with corn meal. 6. They taste good.

Harcourt Brace School Publishers

Word Webs

Before reading an article, create a word web to introduce a vocabulary word or concept. Write the concept or vocabulary word in the center circle of the web and invite children to brainstorm related words or concepts for the other circles. Word webs can be created as a whole-class activity or as small-group activities.

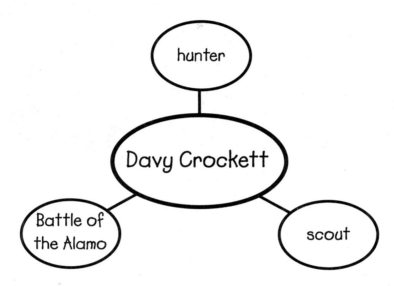

K-W-L Charts

Before reading an article, invite children to create a K-W-L chart like the one below. Children can fill in columns one and two before reading and column three after reading.

What I Know	What I Want to Know	What I Learned
Native Americans used what they found in the land for their homes.	What kinds of materials did the Native Americans of the Southwest use?	Native Americans of the Southwest used the cliffs and mesas to build their homes.

Anticipation Guides

Before reading an article, prepare a set of three statements that children can classify as **agree** or **disagree.** You may wish to write these statements on the board or on an overhead transparency. Then have the whole class come to a consensus about whether they agree or disagree with the statements. After reading, children can discuss how accurate their classifications were.

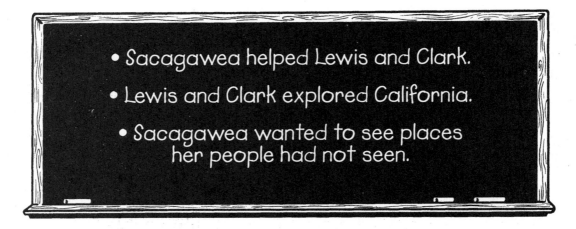

- Sacagawea helped Lewis and Clark.
- Lewis and Clark explored California.
- Sacagawea wanted to see places her people had not seen.

Other kinds of anticipation guides can be developed to focus on vocabulary words or to present statements that children have to make predictions about.

Preview/Prediction Charts

To help children preview an article and make predictions about the content they will read, create a chart like the one below. Model this chart on an overhead transparency or on the board, and invite children to make one like it in their journals or learning logs. Children can record their predictions before reading and verify or revise them as they read.

Prediction	Clues	What Really Happened
People no longer trade goods for goods today.	People use credit cards and money today to trade.	Friends and relatives still trade goods, but most people buy goods with cash and credit cards.

Photos and Illustrations

Remind children that photos and illustrations can help them understand the text on the page. Very often photos and illustrations are used to clarify concepts or vocabulary words that are discussed in the text. Frequently, point out illustrations and photos to children, and ask them to discuss what they see. Use maps provided in the book as well as maps in the classroom to help children gain geographical understandings.

NEW YORK

Outlines

Before reading, children can identify the main idea of a story or article by scanning each paragraph. After reading, they can fill in more details.

Outline

Greetings

A. People send greeting cards.
 1. Cards for holidays
 2. Cards for other special days

B. People in Egypt and Rome sent greetings over 4,000 years ago.

C. Many kinds of cards are made and sold every year.

Flow Charts—Visual Representations

Before, during, and after reading, children can benefit from using visual frameworks, such as flow charts, to organize the text. Visual frameworks can be set up to show how something is done or made. The content of the lesson will dictate what kind of visual framework you develop. The flow chart below works well showing a simple process.

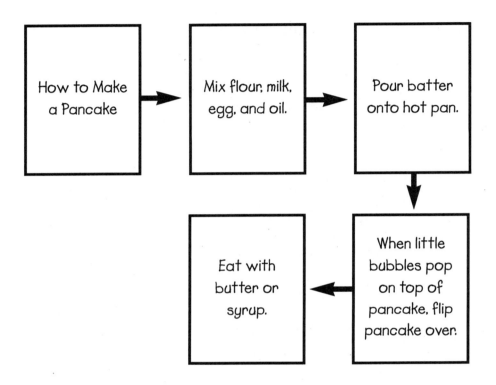

Cause/Effect Charts

Assist children in seeing cause-and-effect relationships by having them create cause/effect charts. After reading an article or a lesson, children can create a chart like the one below.

What Happened	Why It Happened
Davy Crockett was a good hunter.	Davy Crockett's father gave him one bullet a day to hunt for food.
Davy Crockett died at the Battle of the Alamo.	Davy Crockett defended the fort against the Mexican Army.

Hands-On Activity

Many students can benefit from a hands-on experience to reinforce social studies content. The following activity, which allows students to identify the main idea, is a good one to use to provide a tactile experience.

A SOCIAL STUDIES BOOK

Materials:

magazines	crayons or markers	paste
paper	construction paper	yarn
pencils	scissors	three-hole punch

1. For each article have children look through magazines and cut out pictures that have to do with information found in the article.

2. Next, have children paste each picture on a separate sheet of construction paper.

3. Next, have children write above each picture how the picture is related to the article. Children can also write a description of the picture or a story that relates to it.

4. After reading all the articles, children can put the pages together to make a book. Have them make a cover for their book. They can illustrate the cover with original drawings or with pictures from a magazine.

Name_____

Word Web

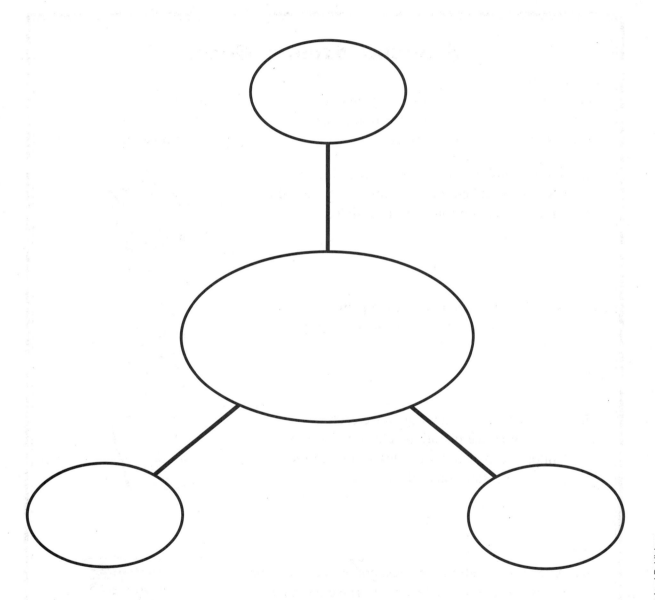

Harcourt Brace School Publishers

K-W-L Chart

What I Know	What I Want to Know	What I Learned

Name_____

Prediction Chart

Prediction	Clues	What Really Happened

Harcourt Brace School Publishers

Outline

A.

    1.

    2.

    3.

B.

    1.

    2.

    3.

C.

    1.

    2.

    3.

D.

    1.

    2.

    3.

Harcourt Brace School Publishers

Name_____

Flow Chart

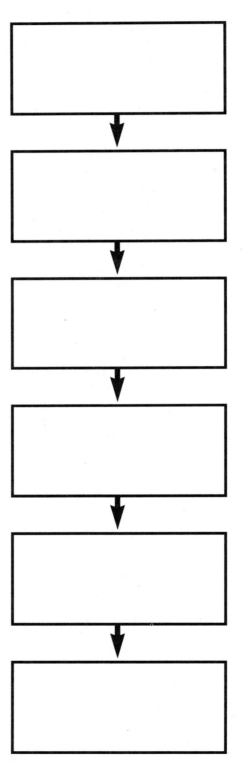

Harcourt Brace School Publishers

Name_____

Cause/Effect Chart

What Happened	Why It Happened